It's Easy To Play Chart Hits.

Wise Publications
London / New York / Paris / Sydney / Copenhagen / Madrid / Tokyo

Exclusive Distributors:

Music Sales Limited
8/9 Frith Street, London W1D 3JB, England.

Music Sales Pty Limited
120 Rothschild Avenue, Rosebery, NSW 2018, Australia.

Order No. AM963259
ISBN 0-7119-8085-3
This book © Copyright 2001 by Wise Publications.

Cover photographs courtesy of London Features International
Compiled by Nick Crispin.
Music arranged by Stephen Duro.
Music processed by Allegro Reproductions.

Music Sales' complete catalogue describes thousands of titles and
is available in full colour sections by subject, direct from Music Sales Limited.
Please state your areas of interest and send a cheque/postal order for £1.50 for postage to:
Music Sales Limited, Newmarket Road, Bury St. Edmunds, Suffolk IP33 3YB.

www.musicsales.com

Your Guarantee of Quality:
As publishers, we strive to produce every book to the highest commercial standards.
The music has been freshly engraved and the book has been carefully designed to minimise awkward page turns and to make playing from it a real pleasure.
Particular care has been given to specifying acid-free, neutral-sized paper made from pulps which have not been elemental chlorine bleached.
This pulp is from farmed sustainable forests and was produced with special regard for the environment.
Throughout, the printing and binding have been planned to ensure a sturdy, attractive publication which should give years of enjoyment.
If your copy fails to meet our high standards, please inform us and we will gladly replace it.

Printed in the United Kingdom by
Caligraving Limited, Thetford, Norfolk.

Don't Stop Movin'

Words & Music by Simon Ellis, Sheppard Solomon & S Club 7

Moderately

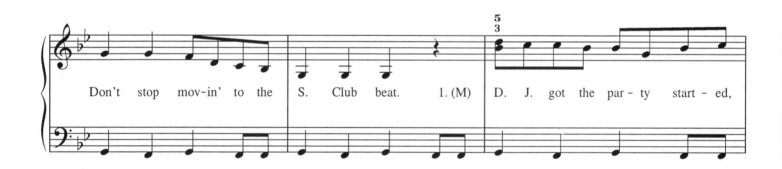

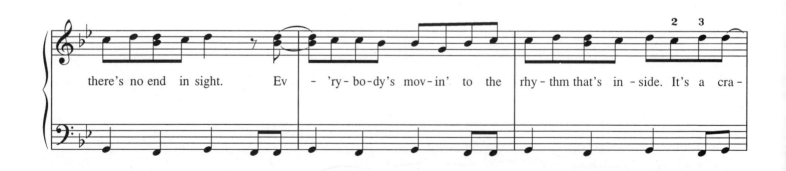

the wait — ing, right here on the dance floor is where you got - ta let it go. Don't—

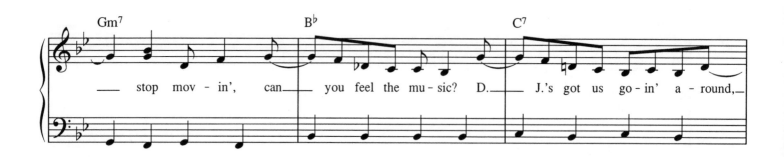

— stop mov - in', can— you feel the mu - sic? D.— J.'s got us go - in' a - round,—

— round.— Don't— stop mov - in', find— your own way to it. Lis -

- ten to the mu - sic. Tak - ing you to pla - ces that you've nev - er been be - fore, ba - by now.

Don't stop mov - in' to the fun - ky, fun - ky beat. Don't stop mov - in' to the fun - ky, fun - ky beat.

No need to rea - son why. Just lis-ten to the sound and it makes you come a - live. Don't

stop mov - in', can you feel the mu - sic? D. J.'s got us go - in' a - round,

round. Don't stop mov - in', find your own way to it. Lis -

- ten to the mu - sic. Yeah, yeah, yeah. Don't - ten to the mu - sic. Tak-

- ing you to pla - ces that you've nev - er been be - fore, ba - by now.

Verse 3:

You can touch the moment almost feel it in the air
Don't know where we're goin' baby we don't even care
Ain't no mystery, just use your imagination
Let it take you there
Just go with your magic baby
I can see it there in your eyes
Let it flow, stop the waiting, right here on the dance floor
Is where you gotta let it go.

Don't stop movin' can you feel the music *etc.*

Eternity

Words & Music by Robbie Williams & Guy Chambers

sing this sum - mer se - re - nade, the past is done, we've been__ be - trayed

it's true.__ Some - one said the truth will out and

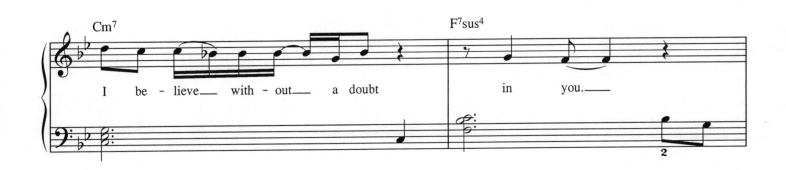

I be - lieve__ with - out__ a doubt in you.__

You were there for sum - mer dream - ing and you

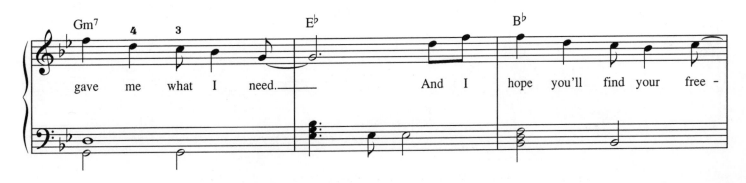

gave me what I need.__ And I hope you'll find your free -

12

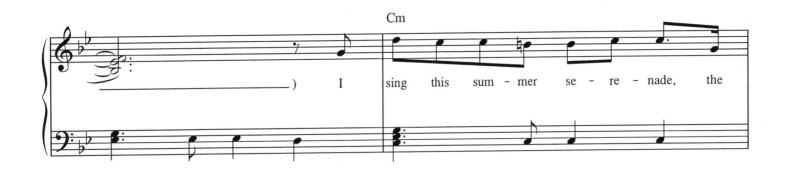

I sing this sum - mer se - re - nade, the

past is done, we've been — be - trayed   it's   true. —

Youth is was - ted on the young be - fore you know, — it's come and gone

too   soon. —   You were

there   for   sum - mer dream   -   ing   and   you

gave   me   what   I   need.   And   I   hope you'll find your free -
2° (know)

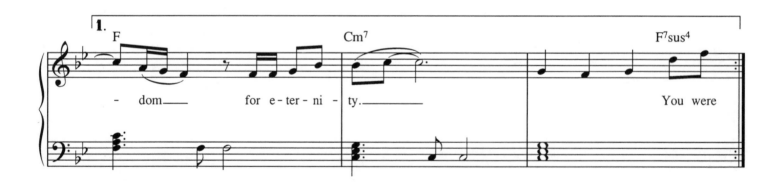

1.
- dom   for   e - ter - ni - ty.   You   were

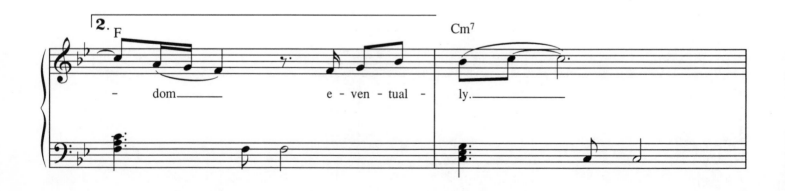

2.
- dom   e - ven - tual - ly.

14

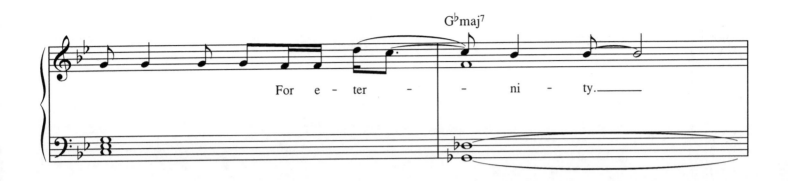

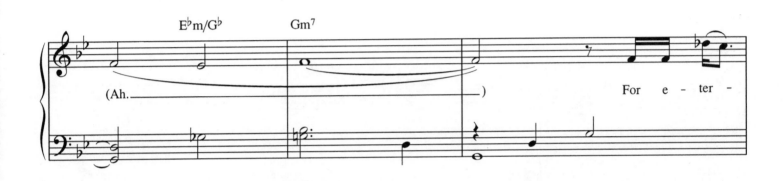

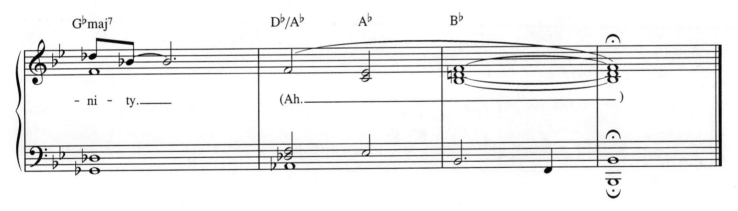

Verse 2:

Yesterday when you were walking
We talked about your Mum and Dad
What they did that made you happy
What they did that made you sad
We sat and watched the sun go down
Picked a star before we lost the moon
Youth is wasted on the young
Before you know, it's come and gone too soon.

You were there for summer dreaming *etc.*

Only For A While

Words & Music by Joseph Washbourn

1. Oh once up-on—— a time, a child—— heard a line—— —— that moved—— —— him.—— The child ne-ver grew,—— —— the line it came—— true—— and all—— a - round.——

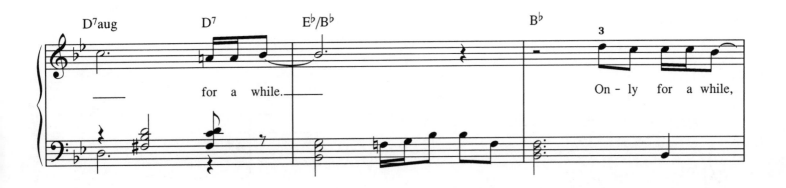

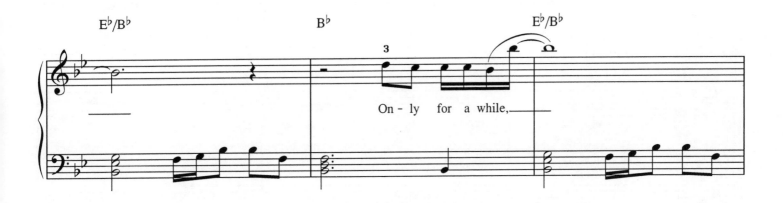

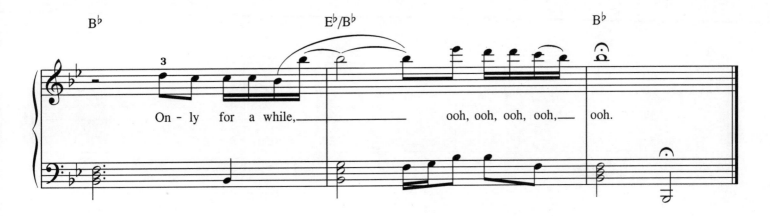

Verse 3:

I know I'll never be able to be free
From these memories
Have love in life the same
Embrace it every day
That it comes to you

Youve got to lie down for a while *etc.*

Out Of Reach

Words & Music by Gabrielle & Jonathan Shorten

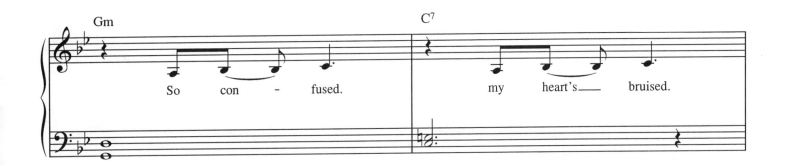

Gm

So con - fused.

C[7]

my heart's bruised.

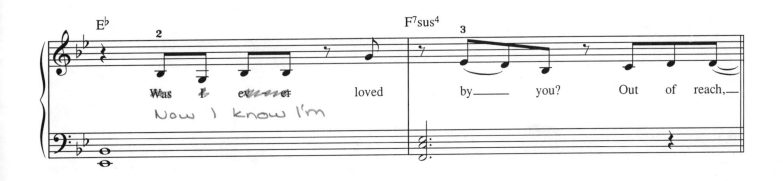

E♭

Was I ever loved

Now I know I'm

F[7]sus[4]

by you? Out of reach,

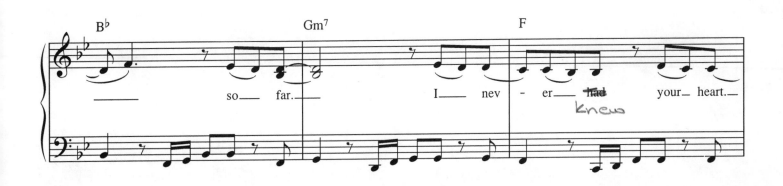

B♭

so far.

Gm[7]

I nev - er had

Knew

F

your heart.

E♭

Out of reach,

B♭

could-n't see.

Gm[7]

We were nev -

This is how

No breath.

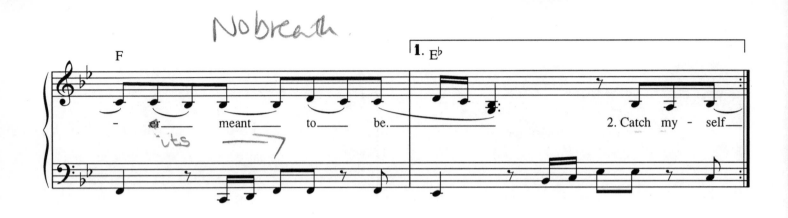

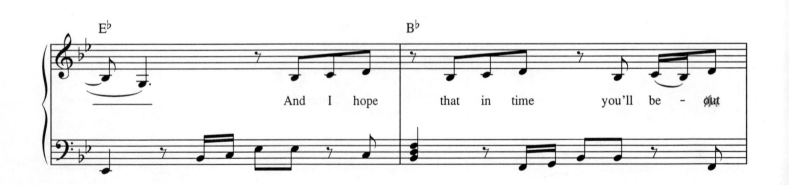

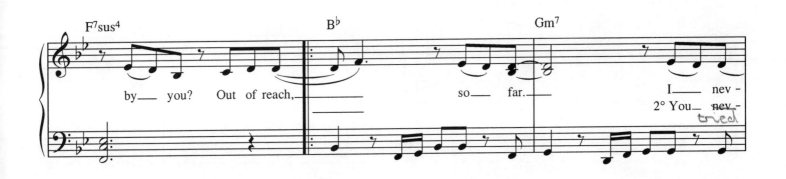

could – n't   see.
I   can   see

This is
We   were   nev –
there's   a   light

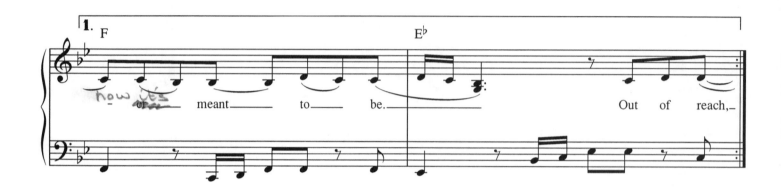

1.   F   E♭

– er   meant   to   be.   Out   of   reach,–

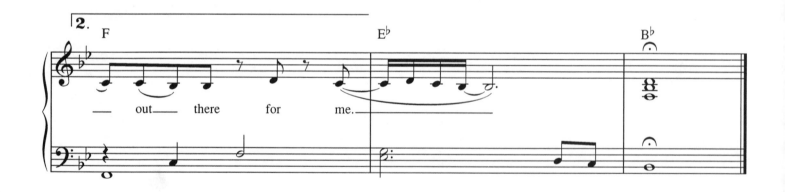

2.   F   E♭   B♭

– out   there   for   me.

Verse 2:

Catch myself from despair
I could drown if I stay here
Keeping busy every day
I know I will be O.K.
But I was so confused
My heart's bruised
Was I ever loved by you?

Now I know I'm.

Out of reach *etc.*

Pure And Simple

Words & Music by Tim Hawes, Pete Kirtley & Alison Clarkson

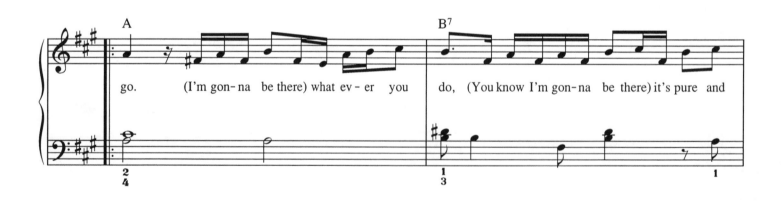

takes, (I'm gon-na be there) I swear it's true,___ (You know I'm gon-na be there) it's pure and

1.

sim - ple, (Oh yeah, yeah.) I'll be there___ for you. (Pure and sim - ple gon -na be there.) Wher-ev - er you

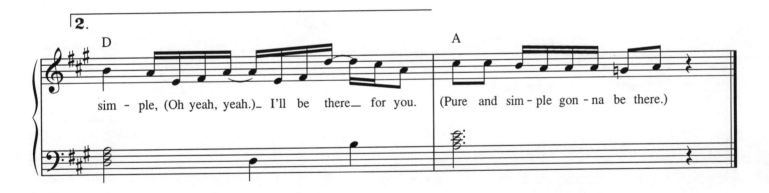

2.

sim - ple, (Oh yeah, yeah.)_ I'll be there___ for you. (Pure and sim - ple gon -na be there.)

Verse 2:

I'll be there through the stormiest weather
Always trying to make things a bit better
And I know I gotta try and get through to you
You can love me in a way like no other
But the situation's taking you under
So you need to tell me now what you wanna do.

I know I've been walking around in daze (Baby, baby)
You gotta believe me when I say (Ah, ooh, ooh)

Wherever you go *etc.*

Walking Away

Words & Music by Craig David & Mark Hill

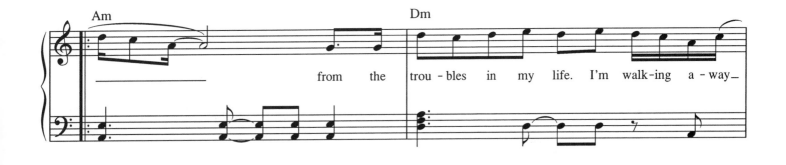

from the trou-bles in my life. I'm walk-ing a-way

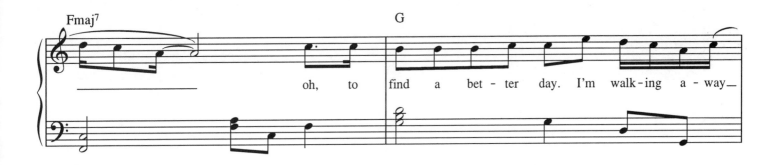

oh, to find a bet-ter day. I'm walk-ing a-way

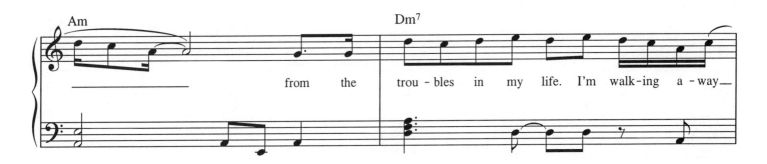

from the trou-bles in my life. I'm walk-ing a-way

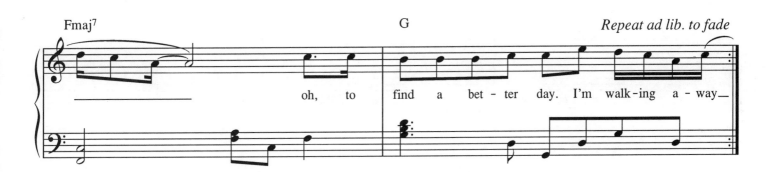

Repeat ad lib. to fade

oh, to find a bet-ter day. I'm walk-ing a-way

Verse 2:

Well, I'm so tired baby
Things you say, you're driving me away
Whispers in the powder room baby, don't listen to the games they play
Girl I thought you'd realise, I'm not like them other guys
'Cos I see them with my own eyes, you should've been more wise, and
Well I don't wanna live my life, too many sleepless nights
Not mentioning the fights, I'm sorry to say lady.

I'm walking away   *etc.*

What Took You So Long?

Words & Music by Emma Bunton, Richard Stannard, Julian Gallagher,
Martin Harrington, John Themis & Dave Morgan

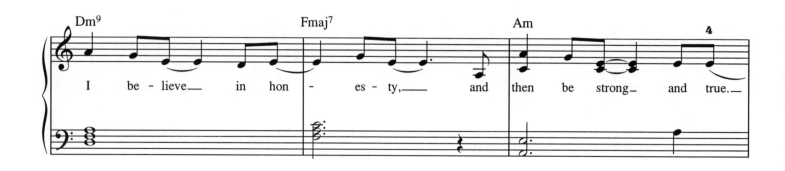

I be-lieve___ in hon - es - ty,___ and then be strong___ and true.

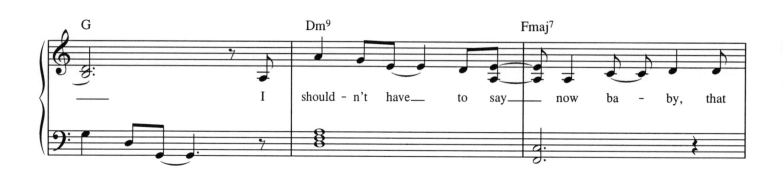

___ I should - n't have___ to say___ now ba - by, that

I be - lieve___ in you.___ What took you so

D.S. (2°) al Coda

CODA

What took you so long? What took you all night? What took you for - ev -

Verse 2:

Oh, you touched my heart right from the start
You didn't know what to say
But honey understand when you take my hand
Everything's okay
'Cause baby I believe reality
It's never far away
I've had enough, so listen baby
I've got something to say.

What took you so long *etc.*

Whole Again

Words & Music by Stuart Kershaw, Andy McCluskey, Bill Padley & Jeremy Godfrey

Moderately

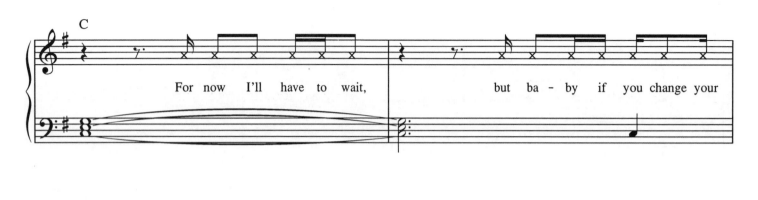

For now I'll have to wait, but ba - by if you change your

mind, don't be too late 'cos I just can't go on, it's al - rea - dy been too

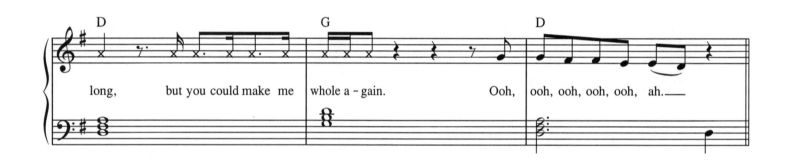

long, but you could make me whole a - gain. Ooh, ooh, ooh, ooh, ooh, ah.

Look - in' back on where we first met, I can - not es -

- cape and I can - not for - get. Ba - by you're the

one, you— still turn me on,— you can make me whole— a - gain.—

1. oh, whoa.— **2.** Oh,— ba - by you're the one,— you— still turn me

on,— you can make me whole— a - gain.—

Verse 2:

Time is laying heavy on my heart
Seems I've got too much of it since we've been apart
My friends make me smile, if only for a while
You can make me whole again.
Lookin' back on where we first met *etc.*

Sing

Words & Music by Fran Healy

sing,   sing,___ sing,___   sing._____   2. Cold___

Ooh._____

Oh,_____   oh,_____   oh.___

Oh,___

3. Ba - by,   there's some -thing   go - in' wrong   to - day,___

but I say no-thing, no-thing, no-thing, no-thing, no-thing,

no-thing, no-thing, no-thing, no-thing, no-thing. So na, na, na, na, now if you sing,—

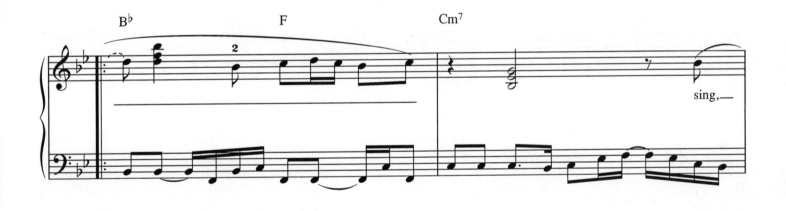

sing,—

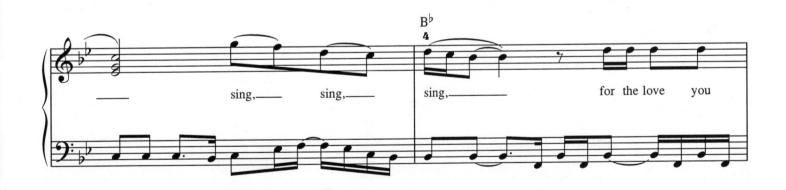

sing,— sing,— sing,— for the love you

bring   won't   mean a   thing   un‑less   you

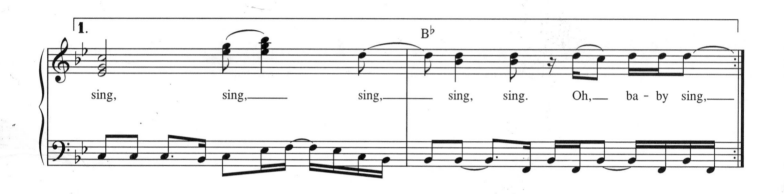

1. sing,   sing,   sing,   sing, sing. Oh, ba‑by sing,

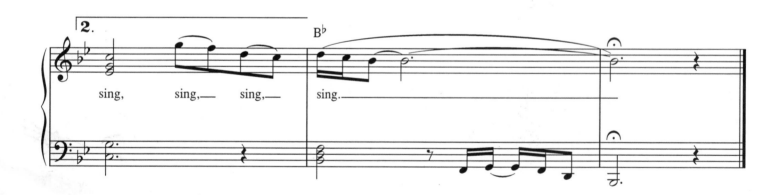

2. sing,   sing,   sing,   sing.

Verse 2:

Colder, crying over your shoulder
Hold her, tell her everything's gonna be fine
Surely you've been going to hurry
Hurry, 'cos no-one's gonna be stopped.

Not if you sing *etc.*